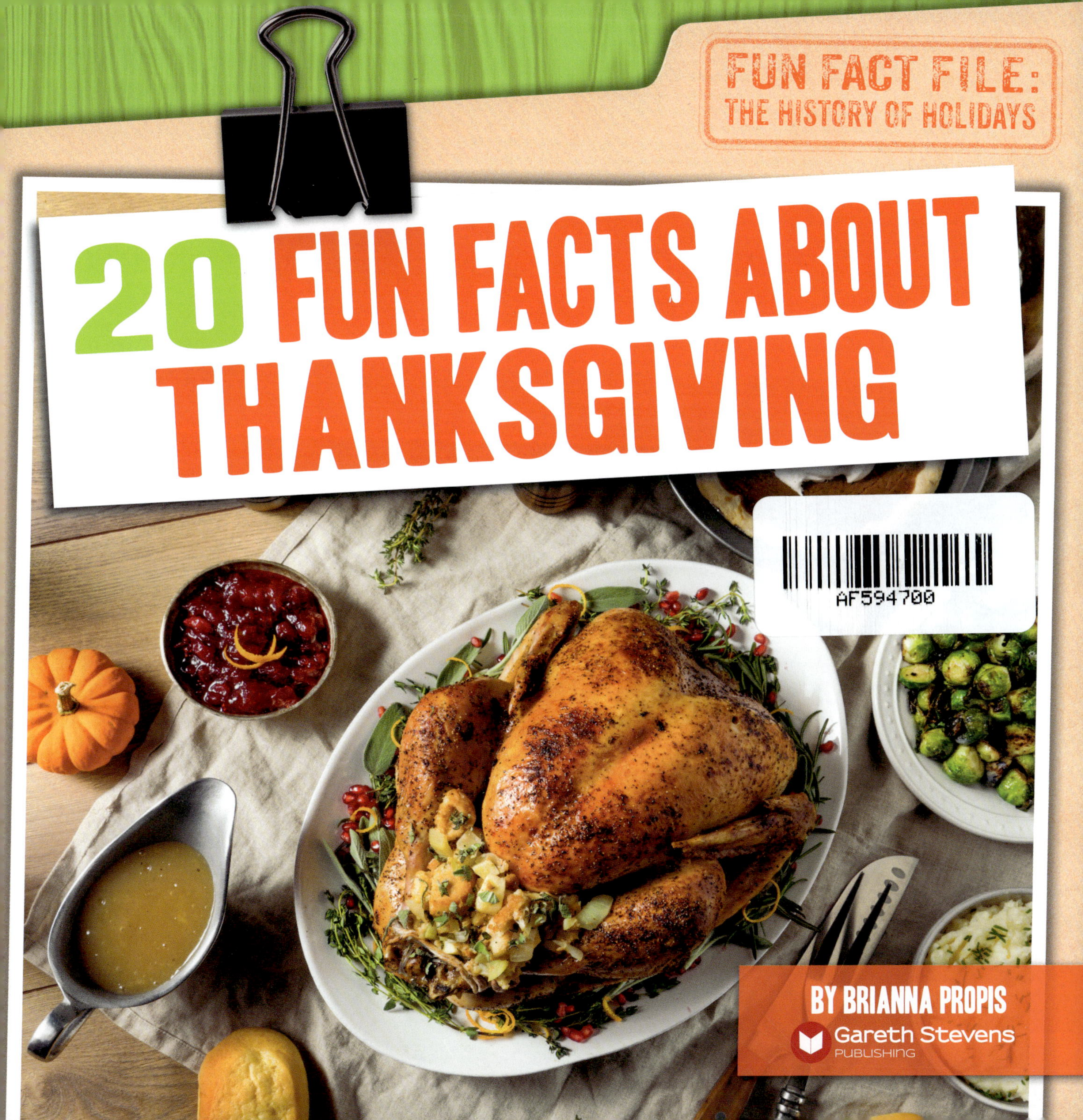
FUN FACT FILE:
THE HISTORY OF HOLIDAYS
20 FUN FACTS ABOUT THANKSGIVING
AF594700
BY BRIANNA PROPIS
Gareth Stevens
PUBLISHING

Please visit our website, www.garethstevens.com. For a free color catalog of all our high-quality books, call toll free 1-800-542-2595 or fax 1-877-542-2596.

Library of Congress Cataloging-in-Publication Data
Names: Propis, Brianna, author.
Title: 20 fun facts about Thanksgiving / Brianna Propis.
Other titles: Twenty fun facts about Thanksgiving
Description: Buffalo, NY : Gareth Stevens Publishing, 2025. | Series: Fun fact file. The history of holidays | Includes bibliographical references and index.
Identifiers: LCCN 2024001377 (print) | LCCN 2024001378 (ebook) | ISBN 9781482466256 (library binding) | ISBN 9781482466249 (paperback) | ISBN 9781482466263 (ebook)
Subjects: LCSH: Thanksgiving Day–Juvenile literature.
Classification: LCC GT4975 .P76 2025 (print) | LCC GT4975 (ebook) | DDC 394.2649–dc23/eng/20240119
LC record available at https://lccn.loc.gov/2024001377
LC ebook record available at https://lccn.loc.gov/2024001378

First Edition

Published in 2025 by
Gareth Stevens Publishing
2544 Clinton St
Buffalo, NY 14224

Editor: Therese Shea

Photo credits: Cover, p. 1 (main) Brent Hofacker/Shutterstock.com; file folder used throughout David Smart/Shutterstock.com; binder clip used throughout luckyraccoon/Shutterstock.com; wood grain background used throughout ARENA Creative/Shutterstock.com; p. 5 Drazen Zigic/Shutterstock.com; p. 6 Squantohowwellthecornprospered.png/Wikimedia Commons; p. 7 Marcio Jose Bastos Silva/Shutterstock.com; p. 8 Olha Yefimova/Shutterstock.com; p. 9 Carey Jaman/Shutterstock.com; p. 10 Erika Anes/Shutterstock.com; p. 12 Everett Collection/Shutterstock.com; p. 13 Franklin D. Roosevelt 1936 june.jpg/Wikimedia Commons; p. 14 President George H. W. Bush at the Annual Presidential Pardoning of the Thanksgiving Turkey.jpg/Wikimedia Commons; p. 15 Sarah Hale in Godeys.jpg/Wikimedia Commons; p. 16 courtesy of the Library of Congress; p. 17 (upper) Phillip van Zyl/Shutterstock.com; p. 17 (lower) thangs1/Shutterstock.com; p. 18 Rudmer Zwerver/Shutterstock.com; p. 19 Brent Hofacker/Shutterstock.com; p. 20 Charles Knowles/Shutterstock.com; p. 21 John Ruberry/Shutterstock.com; p. 22 April Visuals/Shutterstock.com; p. 23 Magali Gomez Paz/Shutterstock.com; p. 24 bbernard/Shutterstock.com; pp. 25, 26 Alexander Raths/Shutterstock.com; p. 27 Chay_Tee/Shutterstock.com; p. 29 View Apart/Shutterstock.com.

Printed in the United States of America

Some of the images in this book illustrate individuals who are models. The depictions do not imply actual situations or events.

CPSIA compliance information: Batch #CS25GS: For further information contact Gareth Stevens, New York, New York at 1-800-542-2595.

Words in the glossary appear in **bold** type the first time they are used in the text.

A TASTY TRADITION

Millions of Americans **celebrate** Thanksgiving every fourth Thursday of November. It's a holiday about spending time with loved ones and cooking and eating a yummy meal. Other fun modern **traditions** include running races and watching football games.

The beginning of this holiday took place long ago. In the early 1600s, British colonists shared their fall crops in a feast with the Native American Wampanoag people. It wasn't called Thanksgiving then, but we trace American Thanksgiving back to this event. Read on to learn more fun facts about this holiday.

About 46 million turkeys are eaten each year in the United States on Thanksgiving.

A HARVEST FEAST

FUN FACT: 1

THE FIRST THANKSGIVING LASTED THREE DAYS.

In September 1620, a group of British people sailed to North America on a ship called the *Mayflower*. They built Plymouth village in today's Massachusetts. In November 1621, these **Pilgrims** invited Native Americans to a three-day celebration of their first harvest, or crops.

Native Americans, including Tisquantum (sometimes called Squanto) of the Pawtuxet band of Wampanoag, taught the Plymouth colonists how to grow and find food. The first Thanksgiving wouldn't have happened without the Native Americans' aid.

At the time of the first Thanksgiving, the sachem, or chief, of the Wampanoag peoples was Ousamequin. The Pilgrims called him Massasoit.

FUN FACT: 2

THE WAMPANOAG LIVED IN THE AREA WHERE PLYMOUTH WAS BUILT MANY, MANY YEARS BEFORE THE PILGRIMS ARRIVED.

In fact, they beat the Pilgrims there by about 12,000 years! The Wampanoag lived in the eastern parts of today's Massachusetts and Rhode Island.

FUN FACT: 3

TURKEY MIGHT HAVE BEEN MISSING AT THE FIRST THANKSGIVING.

The Pilgrims and Native Americans likely ate different birds. Some historians think smaller birds, such as goose or duck, were part of the feast. The Wampanoag guests brought deer meat to the celebration.

Can you imagine Thanksgiving dinner without turkey?

Native Americans used cranberries for food and other purposes, including to color rugs and blankets and to treat wounds and illness.

FUN FACT: 4

CRANBERRIES WERE LIKELY AT THE FIRST THANKSGIVING, BUT NOT CRANBERRY SAUCE.

Cranberries grew wild in the Plymouth area, and the Wampanoag showed the Pilgrims how to prepare them. However, the Pilgrims wouldn't have made cranberry sauce because they had run out of sugar.

AROUND THE WORLD

FUN FACT: 5

PEOPLE AROUND THE WORLD CELEBRATED DIFFERENT KINDS OF "THANKSGIVINGS" BEFORE THE ONE IN 1621.

For thousands of years, Native Peoples celebrated feasts of thanks, such as "Strawberry Thanksgiving" and "Green Corn Thanksgiving." The British also thanked God for a good harvest on certain days.

Some Wampanoag still celebrate Strawberry Thanksgiving to mark the first fruit harvest of the season.

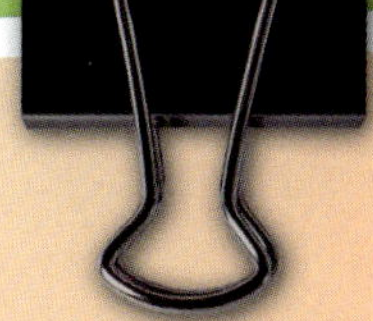

THANKSGIVING CELEBRATIONS AROUND THE WORLD

COUNTRY	HOLIDAY NAME	DATE
CANADA	NATIONAL DAY OF THANKSGIVING	SECOND MONDAY OF OCTOBER
GERMANY	ERNTEDANKFEST ("HARVEST FESTIVAL OF THANKS")	OFTEN THE FIRST SUNDAY OF OCTOBER
LIBERIA	NATIONAL THANKSGIVING DAY	FIRST THURSDAY OF NOVEMBER
JAPAN	KINRO KANSHA NO HI ("LABOR THANKSGIVING DAY")	NOVEMBER 23
NETHERLANDS	DANKDAG ("THANKSGIVING")	FIRST WEDNESDAY OF NOVEMBER

The United States isn't the only country that celebrates Thanksgiving. Many countries around the world have their own special times to give thanks, spend time with loved ones, and eat tasty food.

IT'S PRESIDENTIAL

FUN FACT: 6

THE FIRST DAY OF THANKSGIVING IN THE UNITED STATES WAS IN DECEMBER, NOT NOVEMBER, 1777.

After winning the Battle of Saratoga during the **American Revolution**, General George Washington announced the first U.S. National Day of Thanksgiving would be December 18, 1777.

The Battle of Saratoga was called a turning point in the American Revolution. The U.S. victory resulted in France and other countries supporting the Americans.

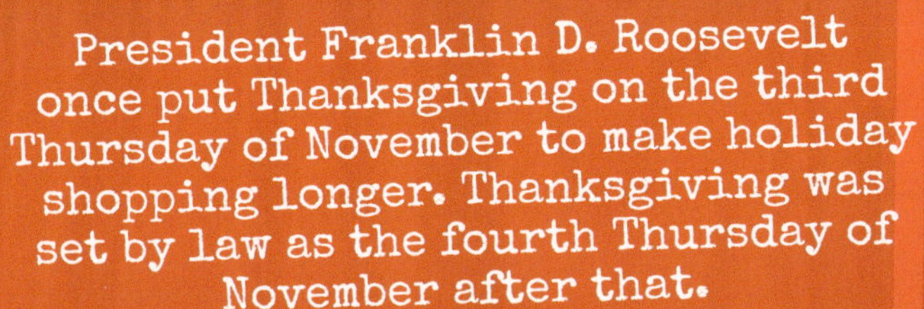

President Franklin D. Roosevelt once put Thanksgiving on the third Thursday of November to make holiday shopping longer. Thanksgiving was set by law as the fourth Thursday of November after that.

FUN FACT: 7

THANKSGIVING WAS OFFICIALLY MADE AN ANNUAL, OR YEARLY, NATIONAL HOLIDAY IN 1863.

President Abraham Lincoln made Thanksgiving a national holiday. During the **American Civil War**, he announced Thursday, November 26, as a national day of Thanksgiving. Nearly every president after also proclaimed Thanksgiving on the fourth Thursday of November.

Presidents have pardoned a turkey or two every year since 1989. To pardon means to officially allow someone to go free, unpunished, after a crime. It's a presidential joke to pardon the turkey.

FUN FACT: 8

SOME TURKEYS HAVE BEEN SAVED FROM THE THANKSGIVING TABLE—BY THE PRESIDENT!

In 1963, a newspaper reported that President John F. Kennedy pardoned a turkey. President George H. W. Bush said a turkey had a "presidential pardon" in 1989. That began an annual tradition.

FUN FACT: 9

THE WOMAN WHO WROTE A FAMOUS NURSERY RHYME HELPED MAKE THANKSGIVING A HOLIDAY.

Thanksgiving was only celebrated around the Northeast United States at first. Hale pushed to make it a national holiday.

Sarah Josepha Hale **published** the children's rhyme we know as "Mary Had A Little Lamb" in 1830. She wrote many letters to the U.S. government asking that Thanksgiving be made a national holiday.

"Jingle Bells" was the first song heard from space! In the 1960s, two astronauts played the song in a message sent to Earth.

FUN FACT: 10

"JINGLE BELLS" WAS A THANKSGIVING SONG!

You may hear it around Christmas now, but "Jingle Bells" wasn't always a Christmas song. The song was published by James Lord Pierpont in 1857. It was then called "One Horse Open Sleigh." Pierpont meant it to be sung for Thanksgiving.

TURKEY TALK

FUN FACT: 11

TURKEY WAS NAMED AFTER THE COUNTRY.

guinea fowl

turkey

Do these birds look alike to you?

Long ago, birds called guinea fowl were sent to Europe from Africa through the land that's now called Türkiye, or Turkey. Europeans began calling these birds "turkey-hens." When Europeans settled in North America, they saw birds like guinea fowl and called them "turkeys."

Both male and female turkeys cackle, purr, and yelp.

FUN FACT: 12

FEMALE TURKEYS DON'T GOBBLE.

"Gobble, gobble" is a funny noise people make to sound like a turkey. But only male turkeys make this sound. Male turkeys are sometimes called "gobblers" because of this call. They use the call to draw the attention of female turkeys.

HOW TO COOK A THANKSGIVING TURKEY

1 TURKEY
1 ONION, PEELED AND QUARTERED
1 LEMON, QUARTERED
FRESH ROSEMARY
FRESH THYME
FRESH SAGE
SALT
PEPPER

1. Preheat the oven to 325ºF (165ºC).
2. Remove the neck and **giblets** from a **thawed** or fresh turkey. Pat the turkey dry with a paper towel.
3. Season the inside of the turkey with salt and pepper. Stuff it with onion and herbs.
4. Have an adult set the turkey on a roasting rack or pan.
5. Spread melted butter over the turkey.
6. Have an adult place the turkey in the oven.
7. Roast the turkey for about 13 to 15 minutes per pound. When the inside of the turkey reaches 165°F (74°C), remove it from the oven.
8. Let the turkey rest about 30 minutes.
9. Cut, serve, and enjoy!

Follow this recipe, or set of steps, to make a Thanksgiving turkey! Make sure to always work with an adult in the kitchen.

The first Swanson TV dinners were heated in the oven. Later meals could be heated in microwaves. They were called TV dinners because they were easy to eat in front of the TV.

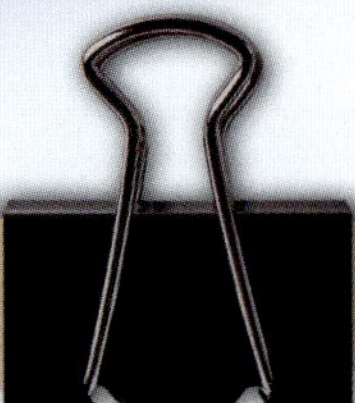

FUN FACT: 13

TURKEY LEFTOVERS LED TO THE CREATION OF TV DINNERS IN 1953.

That year, the Swanson food company had a great many unsold turkeys after Thanksgiving. So, turkey and sides were prepared, placed in trays, and frozen. In 1954, Swanson sold 10 million of these meals!

TOP TRADITIONS

FUN FACT: 14

THE FIRST TURKEY TROT WAS HELD IN 1896.

The turkey trot is the oldest continually run race in North America. In 2022, 756,894 people signed up for turkey trots.

Have you seen people running races on Thanksgiving? Some are called turkey trots. (A trot is a fast pace.) The first turkey trot was held in Buffalo, New York. It was a 5-mile race (8 km).

FUN FACT: 15

THE FIRST ANNUAL NFL (NATIONAL FOOTBALL LEAGUE) THANKSGIVING FOOTBALL GAME WAS PLAYED IN 1934.

That game was between the Detroit Spartans and the Chicago Bears. And Thanksgiving **college** football games go back even further, to 1876. When games began to be played on TV, watching Thanksgiving football became a tradition for many families.

Detroit's pro football team—now the Lions—still plays on Thanksgiving every year.

Snoopy has made the most appearances of any balloon in the Macy's Thanksgiving Day Parade! Since 1968, Snoopy has appeared more than 40 times.

FUN FACT: 16

THE MACY'S THANKSGIVING DAY PARADE ONCE HAD ZOO ANIMALS.

Monkeys, bears, camels, and elephants were featured in the first ever event, then called Macy's Christmas Parade, in 1924. But the parade was too much for the animals to handle. And their roars and growls scared children!

FUN FACT: 17

THANKSGIVING IS A POPULAR TIME TO GO TO THE MOVIES!

Many movies come out on Thanksgiving weekend because people are often off from work and school. Disney's 2013 movie *Frozen* holds the record for most money made on a Thanksgiving opening weekend.

Frozen earned $93.9 million in ticket sales during its first five days in theaters!

A survey is a way of gathering facts by asking people questions. In the 2023 YouGov survey, Thanksgiving was followed by Mother's Day and Christmas.

FUN FACT: 18

THANKSGIVING WAS THE MOST POPULAR U.S. HOLIDAY IN 2023.

Thanksgiving's traditions make this holiday a favorite for many people. In fact, Thanksgiving had the best rating, 81 percent, among adults of all ages in a survey by YouGov, a company that does online studies.

MAKING THE CALL

FUN FACT: 19

PEOPLE CAN CALL CERTAIN TELEPHONE NUMBERS AROUND THANKSGIVING TO ASK COOKING QUESTIONS.

The **U.S. Department of Agriculture** has a phone number for questions about cooking turkey and other meat. The Butterball company has a Turkey Talk-Line. People can call other numbers about baking bread and preparing cranberries too.

One of the most popular questions asked in the Thanksgiving calls is, "How do I thaw a turkey?" This is an important food safety question!

Make sure to toss any food remains in the trash and not the sink, or you may have to call a plumber too! You can remind your family of this as well.

FUN FACT: 20

THE BUSIEST DAY OF THE YEAR FOR MANY PLUMBERS IS THE FRIDAY *AFTER* THANKSGIVING.

Many people call a plumber the day after their Thanksgiving feast. That's because people toss food bits and turkey fat down their sink after the meal. These things can build up and block pipes.

GIVING THANKS

Many people—from Native Peoples to presidents—have shaped American Thanksgiving. The holiday has different forms in different families. Still, most gatherings center on being grateful for loved ones. It's a time of unity, or togetherness.

Sharing a meal to give thanks and celebrate has long been a tradition among many peoples. New traditions will be added to Thanksgiving as the years go by. Your family may already have special traditions. For many, Thanksgiving is a time to put aside differences and celebrate what they're grateful for.

A modern Thanksgiving tradition is to celebrate "Friendsgiving." This is a day when friends get together and share a meal. There's no official date for Friendsgiving, though.

GLOSSARY

American Civil War: A war fought from 1861 to 1865 in the United States between the Union (the Northern states) and the Confederacy (the Southern states).

American Revolution: The war in which 13 British colonies of North America won their freedom from England.

celebrate: To show happiness for an event through activities such as eating or playing music.

college: A school after high school.

giblet: An organ of a bird that can be cooked and eaten as food.

nursery rhyme: A short poem or song written for children.

Pilgrim: An English person who traveled on the *Mayflower* to New England and created the English colony at Plymouth in 1620.

plumber: A worker who puts in or fixes sinks, toilets, water pipes, etc.

publish: To produce a piece of writing or music for sale.

thaw: To become less stiff and frozen after being warmed.

tradition: A way of life or an action that a group of people has practiced for a long time.

U.S. Department of Agriculture: A national agency that oversees farming, ranching, and forestry businesses.

FOR MORE INFORMATION

BOOKS

Hofer, Charles. *Thanksgiving.* North Mankato, MN: Pebble, 2024.

Rathburn, Betsy. *Thanksgiving.* Minneapolis, MN: Bellwether Media, 2023.

Spanier, Kristine. *Thanksgiving.* Minneapolis, MN: Jump!, 2023.

WEBSITES

50 Fun Thanksgiving Facts For Kids
www.mkewithkids.com/post/thanksgiving-facts-for-kids/
Here are many more Thanksgiving fun facts!

National Geographic Kids: The First Thanksgiving
kids.nationalgeographic.com/history/article/first-thanksgiving
Learn more about Thanksgiving's origins.

National Geographic Kids: Thanksgiving Traditions
kids.nationalgeographic.com/history/article/thanksgiving-traditions
Explore some of the most well-known Thanksgiving traditions.

INDEX